BAREBACK RIDING

BY RACHEL GRACK

AMICUS LEARNING

curious about?

CHAPTER THREE

Bringing Home the Win

PAGE

16

Curious About is published by Amicus Learning, an imprint of Amicus
P.O. Box 227, Mankato, MN 56002
www.amicuspublishing.us

Editors: Ana Brauer and Megan Siewert
Series Designer: Kathleen Petelinsek
Book Designer and Photo Researcher: Emily Dietz

Library of Congress Cataloging-in-Publication Data
Names: Koestler-Grack, Rachel A., 1973– author.
Title: Curious about bareback riding / by Rachel Grack.
Description: Mankato, MN : Curious About is published by Amicus Learning, [2025] | Series: Curious about Rodeo | Includes bibliographical references and index. | Audience: Ages 6–9 years | Audience: Grades 2–3 | Summary: "Learn how cowboys and cowgirls compete in bareback riding rodeo events in this question-and-answer book for elementary-aged readers. Includes infographics and back matter to support research skills along with table of contents, glossary, books and websites for further research, and index"—Provided by publisher.
Identifiers: LCCN 2024015019 (print) | LCCN 2024015020 (ebook) | ISBN 9798892000833 (lib bdg) | ISBN 9798892001410 (paperback) | ISBN 9798892001991 (ebook)
Subjects: LCSH: Bronc riding—Juvenile literature.
Classification: LCC GV1834.45.B75 K64 2025 (print) | LCC GV1834.45.B75 (ebook) | DDC 791.8/4—dc23/eng/20240508
LC record available at https://lccn.loc.gov/2024015019
LC ebook record available at https://lccn.loc.gov/2024015020

Photo Credits: Alamy Stock Photo/George Ostertag, 20, 21, Images-USA, 16, Kim Petersen, cover, 1; Dreamstime/ Michele Jackson, 8; Getty Images/eyecrave productions, 6-7, Helen H. Richardson, 9 (*top & middle*), 9 (*second from top*), 9 (*second from bottom*), 9 (*bottom*), Houston Chronicle/ Hearst Newspapers, 19, 11, 2, 10, 13; Getty Images/Rob Carr, 3, 17; Pexels/Dominique BOULAY, 2, 4; Shutterstock/Jackson Stock Photography, 14–15; The Noun Project/Adrien Coquet, 5, Andy Horvath, 22, 23, art shop, 5, Bohdan Burmich, 5, Gan Khoon Lay, 12, HeadsOfBirds, 5, Jason Tropp, 22, 23, Madalyn Jefferson, 5, Oksana Latysheva, 5, Ramesha, 5, Vectorstall, 5

Printed in China

Bareback riding is one of the oldest rodeo events.

What is bareback riding?

It is a rodeo sport. **Contestants** ride bucking horses without saddles or reins. Judges score their performance. Bareback riding is a roughstock event. Each ride must last at least eight seconds. Sound easy? It's not! Bareback riding is hard and dangerous.

WHAT IT TAKES

TIME
Many months on the road

DANGER
Could get badly hurt

COST
Traveling/gear gets spendy

RISK
No win, no pay

WHAT IT GIVES

THRILL
Challenging and dangerous

STAGE
Perform skills for a crowd

COMMUNITY
Form close friendships

CHANCE
Can win a big money prize

A WILD RIDE!

What is roughstock?

These are untamed horses and bulls used in rodeo events. Bareback riders use bucking horses called broncs. They are **bred** and raised to buck. The more a bronc bucks, the better. Bareback riders want a horse that wants them off!

There are people who breed horses to be used in rodeos. Riders prefer horses with stronger bucks.

Why do broncs buck?

Rodeo judges can grant a *re-ride* if the bronc refuses to buck.

It is their nature. Some horses really like to buck. These make good broncs for bareback riding and breeding. Broncs wear a **flank strap** between their bellies and back legs. This makes them buck more. Riders also use their **spurs** to keep broncs bucking.

1 CHAPS

2 GLOVE

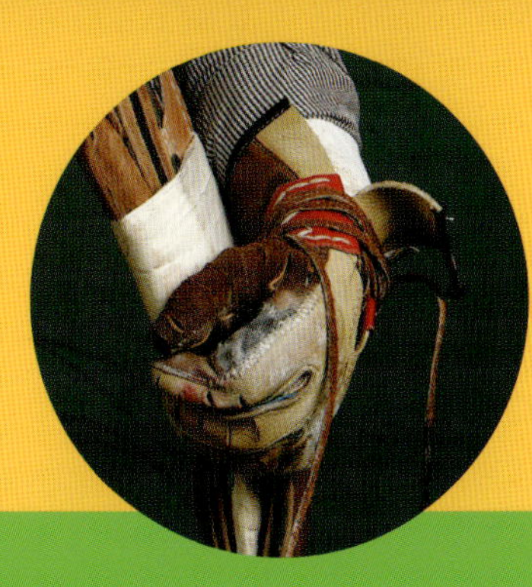

3 HAT

4 BOOTS

5 SPURS

CHAPTER TWO

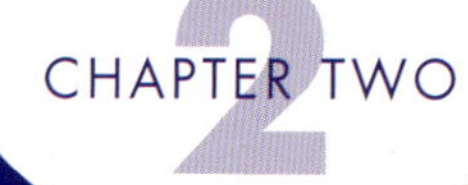

Where do they start?

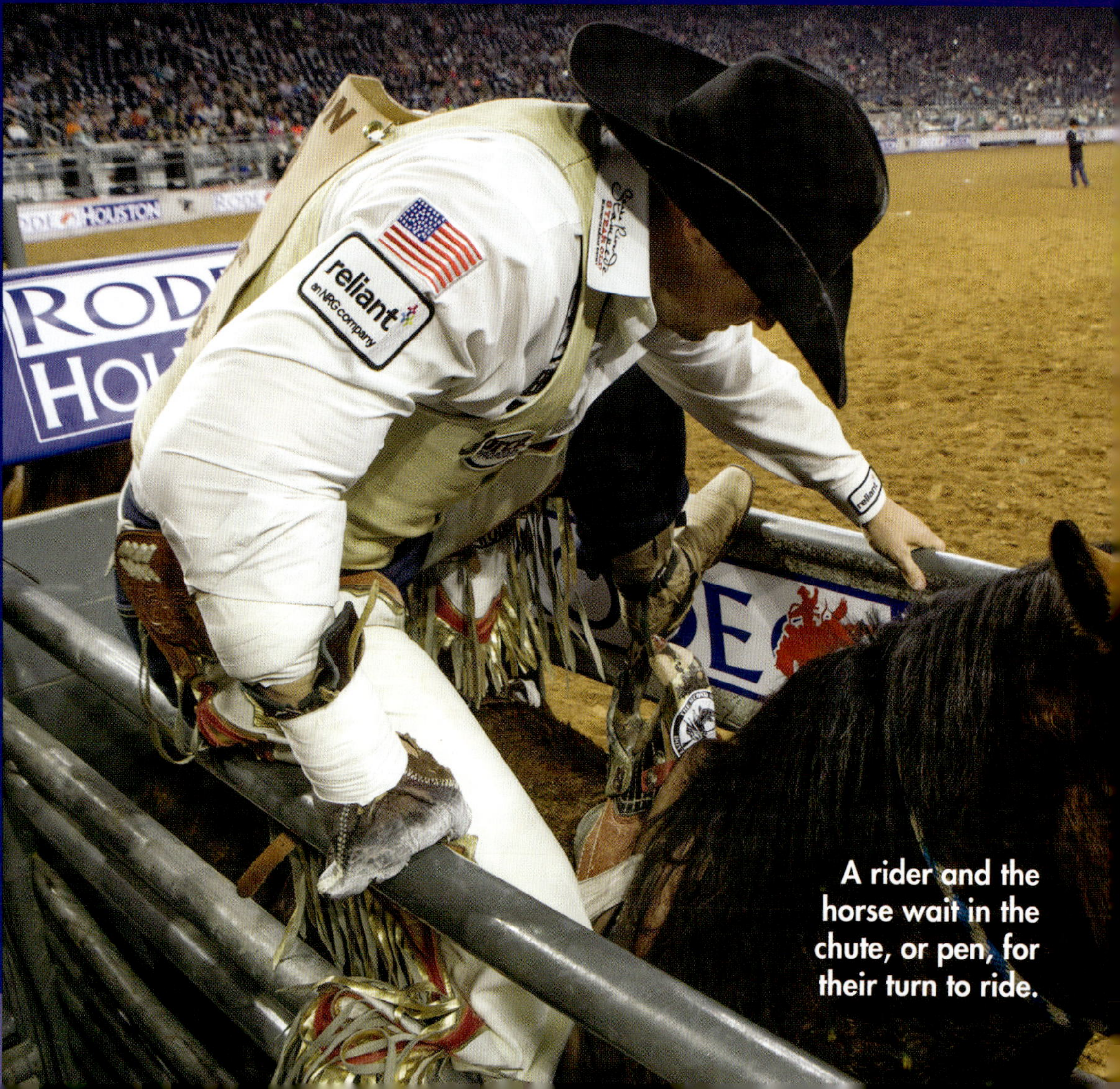

A rider and the horse wait in the chute, or pen, for their turn to ride.

A rider gets on the horse in the chute. Once on, he grabs a hold of the **rigging**. He gets ready to **mark out** the bronc. He stretches out his legs. Both spurs touch the bronc's shoulders. He's ready! He gives the gateman a nod. The chute opens. Hang on tight, cowboy!

The horse takes off running when the gateman (left) opens the chute.

RIGGING

How do riders hold on?

They use the rigging. This handle sits on top of the horse's **withers**. The rigging gets belted around the horse and pulled tight. Broncs twist, jump, and kick. But there's a catch. Riders can only use one hand. It takes a strong grip.

What happens in eight seconds?

Using spurs on a horse leads to stronger bucks.

A lot! The rider leans back. He waves his free hand in the air. He keeps his toes pointed out. His heels stay pressed against the horse. He rolls his spurs up and down the bronc's shoulders. He spurs as long as he can. Every second counts!

Who wins?

Rodeo judges decide who wins each event.

The cowboy with the best score. Judges score both the rider and the horse. They rate the rider's control and spurring action. Broncs get judged on speed, power, and bucking style. Their scores get added together. The highest score is 100 points.

DID YOU KNOW?

In 2021, 18-year-old Rocker Steiner broke the world record for bareback riding with a 95-point score.

What is a "no score"?

Uh-oh. It may mean the rider broke a rule. He cannot touch anything with his free hand. Riders who fail to mark out get a no score. Riders must stay on for at least eight seconds. Was he bucked off? Dust yourself off, cowboy. Maybe next **go-round**!

The rider touches the horse with his free hand. He gets a no score.

It takes a lot of practice
to be a bareback rider.

Could I be a bareback rider?

DID YOU KNOW?
Bareback riders are often cowboys. But cowgirls can ride, too. Some rodeos have roughstock events just for women.

Maybe someday. Youth bronc riding starts around age 14. Check your state's rodeo rules to know for sure. Some states allow mini-bronc riding for younger kids. You could ride a wild pony! Do you think you have what it takes?

ASK MORE QUESTIONS

Is there a rodeo near me?

When can I start bareback riding?

Try a BIG QUESTION:
Could I be a bronc rider?

SEARCH FOR ANSWERS

Search the library catalog or the Internet.
A librarian, teacher, or parent can help you.

Using Keywords
Find the looking glass.

Keywords are the most important words in your question.

If you want to know about:

- finding a rodeo near you, type: RODEO [YOUR STATE]
- youth bareback riding, type: JUNIOR RODEO

FIND GOOD SOURCES

Here are some good, safe sources you can use in your research.
Your librarian can help you find more.

Books

Bareback Riding
by Rochelle Groskreutz, 2021.

Saddle Bronc Riding
by Rachel Grack, 2025.

Internet Sites

Britannica Kids: Rodeos
https://kids.britannica.com/ students/article/rodeo/276762
Britannica is an encyclopedia with educational information on many topics. Learn more about rodeos.

National Little Britches Rodeo Association
https://www.nlbra.com/
NLBRA is a youth rodeo association for kids ages 5 to 18. Visit the website to follow youth rodeo events and standings. Find out if there is an NLBRA location near you.

Every effort has been made to ensure that these websites are appropriate for children. However, because of the nature of the Internet, it is impossible to guarantee that these sites will remain active indefinitely or that their contents will not be altered.

SHARE AND TAKE ACTION

Watch bareback riding.
Ask an adult to help you find videos of bareback riding events. Better yet, go to a rodeo near you!

Take horseback riding lessons.
Bareback riders learn how to ride tame horses first. Get in the saddle, and give it a try!

Attend a rodeo training camp.
Search for rodeo camps in your area and sign up.

bred When animals are mated to get a certain type of offspring.

flank strap A fleece-lined belt placed between a horse's belly and back legs to make it buck.

go-round Riders get more than one round to compete, each ride is a go-round.

mark out When a rider holds their heels on the horse's shoulders until the horse's front feet hit the ground.

rigging A leather suitcase-like handle wrapped around the horse's withers for the rider to hold on to.

spurs The spiked wheels on the heel of a rider's boots.

withers The area between the shoulder blades of a horse.

About the Author

Rachel Grack has been writing children's nonfiction for twenty-five years. She lives on a ranch in the heart of rodeo country (southern Arizona). Some evenings, she wanders over to watch her neighbors in friendly roping competitions. A western restaurant in town offers weekly bull riding and mutton busting. But Rachel much prefers a quiet ride on her gentle paint horse, Lady.